Comptroller of the Currency
Administrator of National Banks

Bankers' Acceptances

Comptroller's Handbook

September 1999

Assets

Bankers' Acceptances

Table of Contents

Background

This booklet is designed to help examiners evaluate bankers' acceptance activities. Some of the booklet's topics are the acceptances':

- Purpose (what they finance).
- Eligibility to be purchased by the Federal Reserve.
- Accounting treatment.
- Risks.

A bankers' acceptance is created when a time draft drawn on a bank, usually to finance the shipment or temporary storage of goods, is stamped "accepted" by the bank. By accepting the draft, the bank makes an unconditional promise to pay the holder of the draft a stated amount at a specified date.

Many commercial traders in the United States and abroad have found acceptance financing a convenient and relatively inexpensive vehicle to finance trade. Although acceptances can be created in any currency, in practice most acceptances are created in the major world currencies such as the U.S. dollar, the Japanese yen, the German mark, and the British pound.

Issuance of Bankers' Acceptances

Process

By far the largest proportion of bankers' acceptances are created as a result of international trade transactions. The diagram in the appendix provides a pictorial summary of an acceptance-generating trade transaction. Following is an example of a bankers' acceptance created by a trade transaction (the numbers in parentheses refer to steps in the appendix's diagram):

NE Trading is interested in purchasing 20 personal computers from Tokyo Tech (1). Since the two companies have never done business with each other, Tokyo Tech will require that NE Trading obtain a letter of credit. The letter of credit places the bank in the intermediary role to facilitate the completion of the transaction.

NE Trading takes the computer purchase contract to its bank, FNB, and makes out an application for a letter of credit (2). FNB opens the letter of credit and sends the original and a copy to Tokyo Tech's bank, Suki Bank (3). Suki Bank staff examines the letter of credit for validity and, upon verifying such, notifies Tokyo Tech. Since Tokyo Tech is not familiar with FNB, it pays a fee to have Suki Bank confirm the letter of credit (4), which makes Suki Bank liable should NE Trading and FNB fail to perform under the letter of credit.

Tokyo Tech ships the goods (5) and presents the shipping documents to Suki Bank (6) to have them negotiated. Along with the documents presented is a draft, drawn on FNB, for the selling price of the goods. (A draft is an unconditional written order signed by one person directing another person to pay a certain sum of money on demand or at a definite time to a third person or to the bearer.) In our example we are using a time draft. The terms of the draft are negotiated at the time the terms of the letter of credit are determined. Suki Bank examines the documents presented and, if they meet the terms and conditions of the letter of credit, it sends the draft and the shipping documents to FNB (7). Had it been a sight draft, Suki Bank would have effected payment of the invoice amount to Tokyo Tech and mailed the draft and documents requesting FNB to credit its account for the amount paid.

FNB compares the documents with the letter of credit to ensure that they meet the terms and conditions stipulated in the letter of credit. If all is in order FNB furnishes NE Trading the documents (8), an advice of amount paid and "accepts" the draft (9). The term "accepted" is stamped on the face of the draft, thus creating a bankers' acceptance. If NE Trading was a large corporation with a market name, it could accept the draft itself without requiring FNB to accept. An acceptance created by a corporation is known as a "trade" acceptance.

By accepting the draft, FNB has accepted Tokyo Tech's demand for payment and commits to pay Tokyo Tech in 90 days. The accepted draft is then sent to Tokyo Tech (through Suki Bank) (10). As part of the letter of credit agreement NE Trading is required to pay FNB within the 90 days (11). The funds are then used by FNB to pay Tokyo Tech (12,13).

Tokyo Tech may hold the acceptance until maturity and present it to FNB for payment, or it may obtain immediate cash by selling the acceptance to an investor, perhaps to FNB or Suki Bank. In the latter case, Suki Bank would then present the acceptance at maturity to FNB for repayment.

Discounting Bankers' Acceptances

When FNB accepted the draft in the example, it acquired an unconditional obligation to pay at maturity a specified amount, either to the Tokyo Tech or to the holder of the instrument if Tokyo Tech discounted the acceptance. If discounted, Tokyo Tech would remain secondarily liable to the holder (purchaser/discounter) of the acceptance in the event of default by FNB.

If FNB purchases (discounts) its own acceptance, it may elect to hold the acceptance in its own portfolio. In this event, the acceptance is recorded as a loan to NE Trading and must be funded like any other loan. More commonly, however, the bank will elect to replenish its funds by selling (rediscounting) the acceptance in the secondary market, either directly or through a dealer. If the bankers' acceptance is not held in portfolio, the bank records its obligation as "acceptances executed."

When an acceptance is sold, ownership is transferred by endorsement to another party termed "holder in due course." The holder in due course has recourse to all previous endorsers if the primary obligor (bank creating the acceptance) does not pay. The secondary obligor (payee on draft) has an unconditional obligation to pay if the primary obligor and the endorser do not, hence the term "two-name paper."

Clean Bankers' Acceptances

A bankers' acceptance may be "clean," i.e., it does not involve a letter of credit. Such acceptances are typically authorized by prior arrangement between the importer's bank and the exporter's bank. In other instances, the draft may be drawn on the seller's bank, or some other bank, particularly if the buyer's bank is small and its acceptances are not widely traded. In this case, the buyer's bank may arrange for another bank — perhaps a larger correspondent bank — to accept the draft and agree to indemnify the accepting bank against any losses that it might suffer in the event of a default. Alternatively, the smaller bank could accept the draft but arrange for a better-known bank to endorse it. In so doing, the buyer's bank retains the credit risk but can offer the buyer access to acceptance financing at a lower cost.

Eligible Acceptances

Section 13 of the Federal Reserve Act of 1913, as amended, (12 USC 372) authorizes the Federal Reserve Banks to discount (i.e., purchase) bankers' acceptances that meet certain eligibility criteria set forth in the statute. The original intent of this provision was to improve liquidity in the market for bankers' acceptances, and thereby to promote the expansion of the United States' foreign trade and commerce. The Federal Reserve also used open-market purchases of bankers' acceptances for many years as an instrument for conducting monetary policy.

To be eligible for discount by a Federal Reserve Bank, a bankers' acceptance must satisfy the following conditions:

- The acceptance must finance a transaction involving the import or export of goods, the domestic shipment of goods, the storage of readily marketable staples, or the creation of foreign exchange;

- The remaining maturity of the acceptance, excluding days of grace, must not exceed 90 days — with an exception for acceptances that finance agricultural trade, for which the maximum remaining maturity is six months; and

- The total amount of drafts that a bank accepts from any one party may not exceed 10 percent of the bank's capital and surplus; the total amount of drafts arising out of domestic transactions that it accepts from all parties combined may not exceed 50 percent of its capital and surplus; and the total amount of drafts of all types that it accepts from all parties combined may not exceed 150 percent of its capital and surplus (unless it receives permission from the Federal Reserve Board to raise that figure to 200 percent).

Bankers' acceptances that satisfy all of these criteria are eligible for discount by a Federal Reserve Bank, and they are also exempt from both the Federal Reserve's reserve requirements and federal lending limits.

Bankers' acceptances whose remaining maturity is greater than 90 days but not greater than six months (or, in the case of acceptances financing the creation of foreign exchange, not greater than three months) are not eligible for discount by a Federal Reserve Bank, nor are they exempt from lending limits. But if they satisfy the other eligibility criteria, they are exempt from reserve requirements.

Drafts accepted for discount by the bank whose remaining maturity is greater than six months (or, in the case of acceptances financing the creation of foreign exchange, greater than three months), or that fail to meet one of the other eligibility criteria, are considered deposits rather than bankers' acceptances under the Federal Reserve Act, and are subject to reserve requirements.

The Federal Reserve stopped using bankers' acceptances as an instrument of monetary policy in 1984, and now very rarely discounts a bankers' acceptance. But the eligibility criteria remain important to banks, for three reasons:

First, as noted above, bankers' acceptances that are eligible for discounting by Federal Reserve Banks are exempt from both reserve requirements and lending limits.

Second, dealers for bankers' acceptances in the secondary market have adopted the Federal Reserve's purchase rules for their own protection, and generally will not discount acceptances that do not comply with them.

And third, eligibility for discounting by Federal Reserve banks provides banks that accept drafts some protection against the possibility of an extraordinary loss of liquidity in the secondary market for acceptances.

Financing Through a Bankers' Acceptance

Bankers' acceptances are used as an alternative to extending a commercial loan to finance an export, for cost or other reasons. In such cases, a time draft covering the financing period is created. A typical example involves a time draft drawn for the amount of the underlying transaction and the desired tenor. The draft is signed and endorsed by the issuing bank on the paying bank. The paying bank accepts the draft, discounts it, and uses the proceeds to make the required sight payment. When the bankers' acceptance matures, it is liquidated in the usual manner by a debit to the account of the opener.

Financing Third-country Transactions

A similar procedure is used when refinancing sight payments under a letter of credit covering trade transactions between three countries. An export from Japan to Bulgaria may, for instance, be payable in U.S. dollars. The American paying or confirming bank would pay the sight draft when it is presented together with required documents. (Actually, the documents would probably be checked and payment made by the Tokyo branch or correspondent of the U.S. bank.) Upon telex advice that documents were presented in Tokyo and payment had been effected, the U.S. bank would create an acceptance. The net U.S. dollar proceeds from discounting the acceptance will be credited to the account of the Japanese branch or correspondent to cover the yen paid to the exporter. One day before the maturity of the acceptance, the Bulgarian issuing bank would supply the U.S. paying bank with sufficient dollars for payment.

U.S. Imports

Bankers' acceptances are also used to refinance imports into the United States under sight letters of credit. In this instance the U.S. opening bank will make payment immediately after the proper documentation and sight draft have been presented. The importer who wishes an additional extension of credit may simply draw a time draft on his or her bank. The latter will accept this time draft and discount it in the usual manner. At maturity of the bankers' acceptance, the importer's account is debited for the amount due.

After the goods arrive, the importer probably will want to take possession of them before making final payment. The bank is generally willing to turn over the documents to the importer if the importer signs a trust receipt. This procedure applies to imports financed by means of a time letter of credit as well as the refinancing of a sight credit on a loan or bankers' acceptance.

Once an exporter has sold the goods to customers and received the proceeds, the importer is required to liquidate any loans or bankers' acceptances that the importer's bank made to finance the specific transaction. If the proceeds of the sale are received before the bankers' acceptance matures, the importer is generally expected to prepay the acceptance. When such prepayments are made, the bank will rebate any unearned discount charges to the customer.

Pre-export

Acceptance financing is also used, by a borrower engaging in international or domestic shipments, to gather, assemble, and pack goods into a quantity sufficiently large for shipment. Under this type of arrangement, the borrower must have a firm export sales order and the term of the pre-shipment financing should be for 30 days or less to be eligible for rediscounting. This means that a bankers' acceptance used to finance a shipment generally should not be drawn more than 30 days before the shipping date (bill of lading date). If a longer period of time is needed, such as to assemble a large shipment of goods, a bank should not extend pre-export acceptance financing beyond 180 days.

Lenders should require borrowers to justify any longer period of pre-shipment financing. They should be wary of using pre-shipment financing to cover a period of manufacturing or other physical transformation of the goods because the draw may be viewed as working capital and considered a loan for lending limit purposes.

Storage

Bankers' acceptances are also used to finance the storage of readily marketable staples in the United States or in any foreign country. To qualify as a "readily marketable staple," a product or commodity must be traded constantly in ready markets with prices quoted frequently enough to make (a) the price easily and definitely ascertainable, and (b) the staple itself easy to realize upon by sale at any time. A bank may only create eligible acceptances to finance storage if the transaction is secured throughout. This means that the financing institution must possess a warehouse receipt or some other document giving it title to the commodities for the entire financing period.

A bank should be aware that bankers' acceptance financing of stored goods should only be used if the commodities are expected to enter into channels of trade in a relatively short period of time. This means that the goods should be promptly sold, exported, or entered into the manufacturing process. They must not be held for speculative purposes.

Although permissible, bankers' acceptance financing is not frequently used for goods stored either domestically or abroad. In domestic trade, borrowers often prefer to finance stored goods by obtaining commercial loans instead of bankers' acceptances. Borrowers who store goods abroad may also be

---

reluctant to use acceptance financing because the legal systems of some countries make it difficult to obtain title to the documents securing the transaction.

Domestic Transactions

Before 1982, bankers' acceptances were only rarely used to finance domestic shipment of merchandise and the storage of readily marketable commodities. Before then, banks were required to have, "shipping documents conveying or securing title" at the time of acceptance. Since most domestic carriers did not issue receipts that met that requirement, domestic trade was usually financed by other means. In 1982, however, Congress amended 12 USC 372 so that the documentary and eligibility requirements for domestic and foreign transactions became similar.

Although the amendment helped increase the use of bankers' acceptances to finance domestic shipments, the total amount of domestic trade currently financed in such a manner remains relatively small. Most domestic shipments are made on open account terms involving no negotiable bill of lading, thereby making the creation of bankers' acceptances impractical.

Dollar Exchange

Dollar exchange bills do not arise from specific trade transactions. Instead, they are used to anticipate proceeds from exports which will be forthcoming within a three-month period. (Twelve USC 373 limits the maximum tenor of dollar-exchange bills to three months.)

Although only a small proportion of total bankers' acceptances outstanding are currently used to create dollar exchange, this type of arrangement benefits a number of foreign countries that rely on one or a limited number of crops for their foreign exchange earnings. Since the export season for these crops is of limited duration, a shortage of foreign exchange may develop just before the start of the season. To overcome this temporary shortage, banks in the exporting country may draw dollar drafts on U.S. banks. The U.S. banks accept the drafts, discount them, and credit the net proceeds to foreign banks. Within three months, the agricultural country should receive foreign exchange as its annual crop is exported. The dollar acceptances can then be liquidated (paid) with the proceeds obtained from the cash crop.

Other Matters of Interest

Working Capital

Bankers' acceptances created to finance inventories or for other working capital purposes not related to any specific transaction are ineligible for rediscount with the Federal Reserve. Banks creating ineligible acceptances for working capital purposes either hold them in their own portfolio or sell them to investors interested in this kind of an instrument. Banks can sell ineligible working-capital bankers' acceptances either directly to investors or through an acceptance dealer. Sometimes known as "marketable deposits," these bankers' acceptances are subject to lending limit restrictions for one borrower (12 USC 84) and therefore must be included with other direct credit extensions to a bank customer.

Prepayment

Since bankers' acceptances are tied to a specific trade transaction, it is possible for the underlying transaction to be completed before the bankers' acceptance used to finance the transaction matures. An importer, for instance, may be able to sell the goods and receive the proceeds well before the acceptance matures. In such cases, most banks require the customer to prepay the bankers' acceptance. Since banks generally are willing to refund a portion of the discount charges in the case of prepayments, the importer saves some expenses. Prepayment also allows the bank to ensure that the proceeds of any transaction it is financing are not diverted to speculative or unauthorized activities.

Even though a bank's customer may be required to prepay a bankers' acceptance, a bank can never prepay or extinguish its own acceptance liability before maturity.

Accounting Treatment

A bankers' acceptance that has been created must appear on the bank's financial statement as a direct asset and liability. The outstanding acceptance is listed as a liability (acceptances executed) and the customer's liability to pay

---

the bank at the acceptances' maturity is shown as an asset (customers' liability for acceptances). If these result from a 90-day letter of credit with multiple transactions, the contingent balance for the letter of credit is reduced when the negotiation takes place and the bankers' acceptance entries are made.

When a bank creates a bankers' acceptance, it receives a fee without advancing its own funds until the acceptance matures. The drawer may hold the bankers' acceptance until maturity, discount it with his or her own bank, or sell it in the acceptance market. If the bank discounts (purchases) its own acceptance, its customers' liability for acceptances (asset) accounts and its acceptances-executed (liability) accounts are reduced and the discounted acceptance is recorded with loans and discounts. In this instance, the bank advances its own funds to the customer. If the bank subsequently rediscounts the bankers' acceptance in the market, that acceptance should be rebooked as customers' liability for acceptances and acceptances executed. A bank's own acceptances, if discounted (purchased), are reflected as loans but, as a practical matter and for accounting convenience, they are not generally deducted from customers' liability for acceptances and acceptances-executed accounts (except for published call and report of examination purposes.)

The customer's liability for acceptances accounts and acceptances-executed accounts may differ only when the asset account is reduced by the customer's prepayment (anticipation) of the acceptance. In that instance, the customer's liability to the bank is reduced by the amount of the payment, but the bank's liability for acceptance (acceptances executed), which is still outstanding in the market, is not reduced. The customer may prepay the bank either the full amount of the liability or any part of it. Customers' funds held to meet acceptances must be considered as deposits and should be reflected as such by the bank, if they are not immediately applied to reduce indebtedness.

Most bankers' acceptances purchased as investments are created by other banks. A bank should report these acceptances at cost under acceptances of other banks on its financial statement and on the call report in Schedule RC-C. The discount should be accreted over the expected remaining life of the acceptance. Bankers' acceptances purchased for trading purposes should be reported in the trading account at market value.

Banks that convey participations in bankers' acceptances to others must report in two sections of the call report. A bankers' acceptance created by one bank that is subsequently participated to another institution is not subject to the 150 percent aggregate capital and surplus limit under 12 USC 372. Such participations between the creating bank and the participating bank are in writing. The participant agrees, for a fee, to assume a portion of the credit risk in the bankers' acceptance. The creating bank that accepted the draft continues to reflect the full amount of the bankers' acceptance in the call report. Both the creating bank's credit risk and 12 USC 372 statutory limits are reduced by the amount of the participation.

Secondary Market for Bankers' Acceptances

When banks sell bankers' acceptances, they use the services of bankers' acceptances dealers/brokers or they go directly to investors.

Bankers' acceptances are not traded on an organized exchange. But a secondary market exists for the acceptances of larger, well-known banks (quotes are available from most securities dealers). "Average" bankers' acceptance yields are published in *The Wall Street Journal*. Since bankers' acceptances are the obligation of the accepting bank, they are traded on the bank's rating. Investors use a tiered approach to pricing that reflects an assessment of the bank's credit standing rather than the class of the bank; i.e., whether it is a money market bank, a regional bank, a Japanese bank, or a Yankee issuer (U.S. dollar acceptances created by foreign banks).

Bankers' acceptances are quoted, bought, and sold on a discounted basis similar to U.S. Treasury bills and commercial paper. Discount rates are obtained from dealers and brokers in New York and other money centers. Some dealers post bid and asked rates, but most trading is done on a negotiated basis. The yields of certain large U.S. banks are quoted as "a run" from one to six months. Bankers' acceptances of "second-tier" banks, Edge Act banks, and foreign banks trade "off the run" (at higher rates).

Brokers do not buy bankers' acceptances for their own account. Instead, they purchase them for resale to investors. Quoted rates reflect an assessment of the underlying draft, which can reflect a number of variables including the perceived credit strength of the bank; the volume of acceptances the bank offers the market; and the amount, tenor, and delivery date of the draft.

Most institutional portfolio managers (and most individual investors) who invest in bankers' acceptances are name-conscious and, as a result, their assessment of a bank's creditworthiness can vary significantly depending on the market's recognition of a bank. In addition, they usually undertake a formal review to develop a list of acceptable banks in whose paper they will invest. Because the strong credits are favored, the resulting demand for their paper gives them a cost advantage over weaker banks.

Volume considerations are also significant. Investors frequently will go to the trouble of qualifying a bank's name only if the bank provides substantial paper to the market. Banks with lower volumes may experience a thinner market and thus incur a cost premium because their bankers' acceptances trade at a higher yield (lower net proceeds upon sale) in the secondary market.

The dollar amount of drafts offered to the market is also important, with investors generally favoring large transactions of $1 million or more. Smaller acceptances and odd amounts can incur a price disadvantage. Bankers' acceptances with maturities shorter than 30 days also generally incur a price disadvantage.

The operational ability of a bank to make timely delivery to the broker of the drafts is important in the secondary market because the broker needs to sell and deliver the acceptances to investors as soon as possible. Convention calls for delivery of drafts and settlement two days after the dealing date. The bank must be able to deliver on the settlement date.

It is not necessary for bank money managers to sell all bankers' acceptances through money center brokers. Frequently, managers can sell their bankers' acceptances locally at a lower yield, which increases the sale proceeds. This is often possible when investors are already accustomed to purchasing the bank's certificates of deposit or other investments. The bank's bond, trust, and retail departments can easily contact local investors without using a broker as an intermediary, thereby reducing cost. Local investors are also more likely to be interested in smaller transactions. Local rediscounting probably best serves to complement rather than replace the broker market, however, because local markets tend to be thin and will not absorb a high volume of paper at the most competitive rates.

Characteristics of Bankers' Acceptances

Credit Quality

An acceptance's credit quality depends on the method by which the bank acquired the acceptance and the acceptance's terms. For an accepting bank, the credit quality is that of the customer whose transaction the bank is financing. The credit quality of a bankers' acceptance may differ from a direct loan depending on the terms and conditions of the two instruments.

When the bank purchases an acceptance in the market, the credit quality is that of the "accepting" bank whose acceptance the bank purchases. Credit quality is also enhanced by the fact that the holder of a bankers' acceptance has secondary recourse to the account party (importer/buyer) in the event the accepting bank defaults.

Marketability

Bankers' acceptances are marketable, short-term investment instruments which are traded actively by banks, brokers, and other institutional investors. Many institutional investors buy and sell bankers' acceptances for their own accounts and for various funds they have established for their customers.

Generally, local investors do not demand the high yields of institutional investors. This increases the bank's acceptance fee when dealing with local investors. Bankers' acceptance rates are based on markets which may move rapidly in a very short time. It is crucial that rates on acceptance financing are available on a timely basis because these instruments have become increasingly volatile. For example, a quote made at 9:30 a.m. may be well off the market at 10:30 a.m. If rates have moved up significantly in that hour, the bank may lose its entire acceptance commission as the funding cost rises. If rates fall during that hour, another bank will almost certainly get the business by lowering its quotation.

Liquidity

Bankers' acceptances are often created to mature in six months or less. Banks can purchase, discount, and sell the acceptances of other banks as short-term, money-market assets (with low risk). Should a bank need to obtain funds, the bankers' acceptances can readily be sold at a predictable price as long as credit quality has not changed.

Risks Associated with Bankers' Acceptances

For purposes of the OCC's discussion of risk, the OCC can be said to assess banking risk relative to its impact on capital and earnings. From a supervisory perspective, risk is the potential that events, expected or unexpected, may have an adverse impact on a bank's earnings or capital. The OCC has defined nine categories of risk for bank supervision purposes.   These risks are credit, interest rate, liquidity, price, foreign currency translation, transaction, compliance, strategic, and reputation.

The risks associated with bankers' acceptances are transaction, compliance, credit, liquidity, foreign currency translation, and reputation. These risks are discussed more fully in the following paragraphs. (Once an examiner determines whether the bankers' acceptances are held as a loan or investment, they should refer to the appropriate booklet in the *Comptroller's Handbook* for further guidance.)

Transaction Risk

Transaction risk is the current and prospective risk to earnings and capital arising from fraud, error, and the inability to deliver products or services, maintain a competitive position, and manage information. Risk is inherent in efforts to gain strategic advantage, and in the failure to keep pace with changes in the financial services marketplace. Transaction risk is evident in each product and service offered. Transaction risk encompasses product development and delivery, transaction processing, systems development, computing systems, complexity of products and services, and the internal control environment.

Banks should work closely with borrowers seeking bankers' acceptance financing to ensure that the borrower fully understands the supporting documentation and timely processing requirements related to this type of financing. The basic documentation for a bankers' acceptance consists of:

- A bankers' acceptance credit agreement which contains the borrower's promise to repay the bank when the acceptance matures.

- A "purpose statement" or letter from the borrower that describes the underlying trade transaction being financed, certifies that no other financing is outstanding, and specifies that the transaction has not been refinanced.

- A draft.

Compliance Risk

Compliance risk is the current and prospective risk to earnings or capital arising from violation of, or nonconformance with, laws, rules, regulations, prescribed practices, internal policies and procedures, or ethical standards. Compliance risk also arises in situations where the laws or rules governing certain bank products or activities of the bank's clients may be ambiguous or untested. This risk exposes the institution to fines, civil money penalties, payment of damages, and the voiding of contracts. Compliance risk can lead to diminished reputation, reduced franchise value, limited business opportunities, reduced expansion potential, and lack of contract enforceability.

The major compliance risk associated with bankers' acceptance financing relates to creating ineligible bankers' acceptances but treating them as if they were eligible for Federal Reserve discount. If this occurs, the Federal Reserve will generally impose a retroactive reserve requirement on the accepting bank. If the bank has created a bankers' acceptance based upon accurate information provided by the borrower in the purpose statement, only to learn later that it erroneously considered the transaction eligible, the bank will not be able to collect compensation from the customer to cover the reserves.

Compliance with the legal lending limit must be considered. When a bank discounts or holds its own bankers' acceptances, they are converted to a loan and included in the legal lending limit. Purchased bankers' acceptances are exempt.

Credit Risk

Credit risk is the current and prospective risk to earnings or capital arising from an obligor's failure to meet the terms of any contract with the bank or otherwise to perform as agreed. Credit risk is found in all activities where success depends on counterparty, issuer, or borrower performance. It arises any time bank funds are extended, committed, invested, or otherwise exposed through actual or implied contractual agreements, whether reflected on or off the balance sheet.

Bankers' acceptances contain credit risk not only for the bank creating the acceptance, but also for the exporter, for banks purchasing another bank's acceptances, and for other investors (such as money market mutual funds, trust departments, state and local governments, insurance companies, pension funds, corporations, and commercial banks) who buy bankers' acceptances.

The principal credit risk of this instrument is that the importer will be unable to make payment at maturity of the bankers' acceptance — leaving the accepting bank responsible to make payment. For acceptances purchased in the market, credit risk is somewhat mitigated because bankers' acceptances are considered to be "two-name paper," which means that the importer is secondarily liable on the instrument. In addition, the instrument is a contingent obligation of the drawer (exporter). In other words, the exporter (drawer) is contingently liable if the importer does not pay. The acceptance is also an obligation of any other institutions that have endorsed it. That is, "holders in due course" that have bought and sold the acceptance in the market.

Liquidity Risk

Liquidity risk is the current and prospective risk to earnings or capital arising from a bank's inability to meet its obligations when they come due without incurring unacceptable losses. Liquidity risk includes the inability to manage unplanned decreases or changes in funding sources. Liquidity risk also arises from the failure to recognize or address changes in market conditions that affect the ability to liquidate assets quickly and with minimal loss in value.

Partly because the maturities of most bankers' acceptances are short, the market generally views acceptances as safe and liquid. The fact that "name" banks dominate acceptance financing also limits liquidity risk. Liquidity risk will be greater if the accepting bank is lower rated, is not a "name" or "prime" institution, or if the instrument is not eligible for Federal Reserve discount.

Foreign Currency Translation Risk

Foreign currency translation risk is the current and prospective risk to capital or earnings arising from the conversion of a bank's financial statements from one currency into another. It refers to the variability in accounting values for a bank's equity accounts that result from variations in exchange rates which are used in translating carrying values and income streams in foreign currencies to U.S. dollars. Market-making and position-taking in foreign currencies should be captured under price risk.

Bankers' acceptances created in foreign currencies, i.e., not in U.S. dollars, are subject to foreign exchange dealing and position-taking risk. The risk to earnings or capital is from movement of foreign exchange rates versus the U.S. dollar. (See the "Foreign Exchange" section of the *Comptroller's Handbook* for guidance on hedging techniques for foreign-denominated bankers' acceptances.)

Reputation Risk

Reputation risk is the current and prospective impact on earnings and capital arising from negative public opinion. This affects the institution's ability to establish new relationships or services or to continue servicing existing relationships. This risk may expose the institution to litigation, financial loss, or a decline in its customer base. Reputation risk exposure is present throughout the organization and includes the responsibility to exercise an abundance of caution in dealing with customers and the community.

In bankers' acceptance activities, a bank lends its good name to a transaction. Therefore, it is important that the customer requesting the bankers' acceptance transaction have a sound reputation. As for the banks, bankers' acceptances are generally created only by reputable, well-known banks with a good credit standing, thus making such instruments safe.

General Procedures

Objective: To determine the scope and objectives of the examination of bankers' acceptances.

1. Review the following OCC documents to identify any previous issues with bankers' acceptances that require follow-up:

    ☐ Previous examination reports.
    ☐ Working papers from previous examinations.
    ☐ Supervisory strategy and overall summary comments.
    ☐ Scope memorandum issued by the bank examiner in charge (EIC).

2. Obtain and review the following bank documents to identify significant changes in bankers' acceptance activity since the previous examination:

    ☐ Internal bank reports management uses to supervise the bankers' acceptance department.
    ☐ Previous internal/external auditor and loan review reports covering the bankers' acceptance department, if any.
    ☐ Any reports and the written policies on insider issues, including codes of ethics and conflict of interest policies.

3. Discuss with management their strategies, objectives, and plans for the bankers' acceptance department.

4. Using information from the previous steps, as well as discussions with the EIC and other appropriate supervisors, determine the scope and objectives of this examination.

Note: Select from the following examination procedures the necessary steps to meet the examination objectives. Seldom will it be necessary to perform all of the steps in an examination.

Quantity of Risk

Conclusion: The quantity of risk is (low, moderate, high).

Objective: To determine the level of risk in the bankers' acceptance portfolio.

1. Using the appropriate sampling technique, select borrowers from the bankers' acceptance trial balance for examination.

2. For all borrowers selected, prepare credit line sheets. Include the borrower's aggregate bankers' acceptance liability and the following information for each bankers' acceptance:

   - Original amount of the acceptance.
   - Current balance of the acceptance indicating any prepayments (anticipations) and portions sold under a participation certificate.
   - Date the acceptance was created.
   - Tenor of the acceptance (give exact maturity date, if specified).
   - Type of acceptance:
     - Import.
     - Export.
     - Third-country shipment.
     - Domestic shipment.
     - Storage.
     - To create foreign exchange.
     - Working capital and/or pre-export.
     - Refinancing of sight letters of credit.
   - Current status of the acceptance.

3. Obtain and review schedules on the following from the examiner assigned "Loan Portfolio Management" if they are applicable to the bankers' acceptance department and may necessitate inclusion of additional borrowers in the credit review:

   - Delinquencies.
   - Participations purchased and sold (conveyed).
   - Acceptance participations sold (conveyed).

- Acceptance pool participations.
- Loan commitments and other contingent liabilities.
- Extensions of credit to major stockholders, officers, directors, and their interests.
- Extensions of credit to employees, officers, and directors of other banks.
- Miscellaneous loan debit and credit suspense accounts.
- Shared national credits (including applicable foreign credits).
- Interagency Country Exposure Review Committee (ICERC) credits.
- Extensions of credit considered "problem loans" by management.
- Information on directors, executive officers, principal shareholders, and their interests.
- Specific guidelines in the lending policy pertaining to the bankers' acceptances.
- Each officer's current lending authority.
- The current fee structure.
- Any useful information resulting from the review of the minutes of the loan and discount committee or any similar committee.
- Reports furnished to the loan and discount committee or any similar committee.
- Reports furnished to the directorate.
- Loans criticized during the previous examination.
- A listing of rebooked charged-off loans (arising from bankers' acceptance transactions).

4. Transcribe or compare information from the schedules described above to credit line sheets, when appropriate, and indicate any past-due status.

- For bankers' acceptances included in the "Shared National Credit Program," transcribe appropriate information from the schedule to the line sheets and return the schedule. (No further examination procedures are necessary.)

- For bankers' acceptances that are covered by an Interagency Country Exposure Review Committee (ICERC) classification, transcribe appropriate information from the schedule to the line sheets, and return the schedule. (No further examination procedures are necessary.)

- For bankers' acceptances criticized during the previous examination, transcribe the:

  - Current balance and payment status, or
  - Date the bankers' acceptance was repaid and the source of repayment.

5. Prepare credit line sheets for any borrower not in the sample which, based on information derived from the schedules described in step 3, requires in-depth review.

6. Obtain liability and other information on common borrowers from examiners assigned to review cash items, overdrafts, and other loan areas, and mutually decide who will review the borrowing relationship.

7. Review credit files for all borrowers for whom credit line sheets were prepared and assess the credit risk. To analyze the loans, do the following:

   - Analyze balance sheet and profit and loss items as reflected in current and preceding financial statements, and determine the existence of any unfavorable trends.
   - Relate items or groups of items in the current financial statements to other items or groups of items set forth in the statements, and determine the existence of any favorable or adverse ratios.
   - Review components of the balance sheet as reflected in the current financial statements, and determine the reasonableness of each item as it relates to the total financial structure.
   - Review supporting information for the major balance sheet items and the techniques used in consolidation. Determine the primary sources of repayment, and evaluate their adequacy.

- Review compliance with the provisions of acceptance agreements.
- Review the digest of officers' memoranda, mercantile reports, credit checks, and correspondence to determine the existence of any problems which might deter the contractual liquidation program.
- Relate any collateral values to outstanding debt, including "margin" and "cash collateral" deposits.
- Compare fees charged to the fee schedules, and determine whether the terms are within established guidelines.
- Compare the amount of bankers' acceptances outstanding with the lending officer's authority.
- Analyze secondary support afforded by guarantors.
- Assess compliance with the bank's established bankers' acceptance policy.

8. For borrowers displaying credit weaknesses or suspected of having additional liability in loan areas, check the central liability file for additional credit relationships.

9. During the file review, transcribe significant liability and other information on officers, principals, and affiliations of borrowing entities. Cross-reference line sheets, when appropriate.

Miscellaneous Credit Procedures

1. Review charged-off loans arising from bankers' acceptance transactions to determine whether loans have been rebooked in contravention of GAAP.

2. For participations purchased and sold:

   - Test participation certificates and records to determine whether the parties share in the risks and contractual payments on a pro rata basis.
   - Determine whether the bank's books and records properly reflect the bank's liability.
   - Investigate any participations sold immediately before the date of examination to determine whether any were sold to avoid possible criticism during the examination.

3.	For acceptance participations (pool participations), determine whether the purchaser has recourse to the bank in the event of default by the account party through either:

- Repurchase agreement, or
- Bank's acknowledgment of its liabilities as guarantor or endorser under the Uniform Commercial Code.

4.	For bankers' acceptances created for officers and directors of other banks, investigate any circumstances that indicate preferential treatment. Prepare a "Report of Borrowings of Officers of Other Banks," if appropriate.

5.	For miscellaneous loan debit and credit suspense accounts, discuss with management any large or old items relating to bankers' acceptances. Perform additional procedures, as appropriate.

6.	Reconcile the bankers' acceptance trial balance to department controls and the general ledger. Review reconciling items for reasonableness.

Objective: To assess compliance with laws, regulations, and rulings relating to bankers' acceptance financing.

Assess compliance with laws, regulations, and rulings relating to bankers' acceptance financing by determining:

- Whether any acceptances have been issued on behalf of an affiliate that would constitute extensions of credit under 12 USC 371c (on transactions with affiliates).
- Compliance with 12 USC 372, which limits the aggregate amount of acceptances outstanding and the amount of acceptances that may be created for any one customer.
- Compliance with 12 USC 373 (on acceptance of drafts for furnishing foreign exchange) by:
	- Identifying acceptances issued to furnish dollar exchange.

- Determining whether those acceptances comply with the prescribed limits.
- The applicability of 12 CFR 7.1007 to bankers' acceptances used in financing credit transactions.
- Which acceptances are "ineligible" under 12 CFR 32.3(c)(2) and therefore subject to 12 USC 84.
- Whether all of the banks' own acceptances discounted (purchased), both eligible and ineligible, are booked as "loans," making them subject to 12 USC 84.
- Whether acceptances of other banks purchased are of the kinds described in 12 USC 372 and 373 (i.e., they are eligible acceptances, and are therefore not subject to any limit based on capital and surplus).
- Whether ineligible acceptances are included within the purchasing bank's 12 USC 84 lending limit to each acceptor bank.
- Whether a bankers' acceptance conveyed through a participation to a junior bank has been excluded from the senior bank's aggregate limits per 12 CFR 250.165.

Quality of Risk Management

**Conclusion: The quality of risk management is
(strong, satisfactory, weak).**

Policy

Conclusion: The board (has/has not) established effective policies governing
bankers' acceptances.

Objective: To assess the adequacy of the bankers' acceptance policy.

1. Determine whether the board of directors, consistent with its duties and
    responsibilities, has adopted bankers' acceptance policies that:

    •   Define the types of acceptances offered and designate qualified
        customers.
    •   Establish procedures for reviewing and approving bankers'
        acceptance applications.
    •   Establish minimum standards for documentation in accordance
        with the Uniform Commercial Code.

2. Determine whether the board or other appropriate committee
    periodically reviews the policies for compatibility with changing market
    conditions.

Processes

Conclusion: Management and the board (have/have not) established effective
processes to manage bankers' acceptances.

Objective: To assess the effectiveness of processes, including internal controls, to
manage bankers' acceptances.

1. Review processes pertaining to underwriting:

- Is appropriate credit analysis performed on the customer (i.e., the buyer/importer) before the transaction?
- Have lines of credit (or credit limits) been established for the foreign banks for which the bank creates acceptances?
- Are credit analyses periodically performed on these banks?
- Are risk reviews performed on the countries in which these banks are domiciled?

2. Review processes pertaining to records:

- Is the preparation and posting of subsidiary bankers' acceptance records performed or reviewed by persons who do not also:
  - Issue official checks or drafts singly?
  - Handle cash?
- Are the subsidiary bankers' acceptance records balanced daily with the appropriate general ledger accounts and are reconciling items adequately investigated by persons who do not normally handle acceptances and post records?
- Are acceptance delinquencies prepared for and reviewed by management in a timely manner?
- Are inquiries about acceptance balances received and investigated by persons who do not normally handle settlements or post records?
- Are bookkeeping adjustments checked and approved by an appropriate officer?
- Is a daily record maintained summarizing acceptance transaction details, e.g., bankers' acceptances created, payments received, and fees collected to support applicable general ledger account entries?
- Are acceptances of other banks that have been purchased in the open market segregated on the bank's records from the bank's own acceptances created?
- Are prepayments (anticipations) on outstanding bankers' acceptances netted against the appropriate asset account, "Customer Liability for Acceptances," (or loans and discounts, depending upon whether or not the bank has discounted its own acceptance), and do they continue to be shown as a bank liability, "acceptances executed"?
- Are bankers' acceptance record copy and liability ledger trial balances prepared and reconciled monthly with control accounts

by employees who do not process or record acceptance transactions?

3. Review the processes pertaining to fees:

    *   Is the preparation and posting of fees and discounts performed or reviewed by persons who do not also:
        *   Issue official checks or drafts singly?
        *   Handle cash?
    *   Are any independent fee and discount computations made and compared or adequately tested to initial fee and discount records by persons who do not also:
        *   Issue official checks or drafts singly?
        *   Handle cash?

4. Review the processes pertaining to collateral:

    *   Are multicopy, prenumbered records maintained that:
        *   Detail the complete description of collateral pledged?
        *   Are typed or completed in ink?
        *   Are signed by the customer?
        *   Are designed so that a copy goes to the customer?
    *   Are the functions of receiving and releasing collateral to borrowers and of making entries in the collateral register performed by different employees?
    *   Is negotiable collateral held under joint custody?
    *   Are receipts obtained and filed for released collateral?
    *   Are securities and commodities valued and margin requirements reviewed at least monthly?
    *   When the support rests on the cash surrender value of insurance policies, is a periodic accounting received from the insurance company and maintained with the policy?
    *   Is a record maintained of entry to the collateral vault?
    *   Are stock powers filed separately to bar negotiability and to deter abstraction of both the security and the negotiating instrument?
    *   Are securities out for transfer, exchange, etc., controlled by prenumbered temporary vault-out tickets?
    *   Has the bank instituted a system which ensures that:
        *   Security agreements are filed?
        *   Collateral mortgages are properly recorded?

- • Title searches and property appraisals are performed in connection with collateral mortgages?
- • Insurance coverage (including loss payee clause) is in effect on property covered by collateral mortgages?
- Are coupon tickler cards set up covering all coupon bonds held as collateral?
- Are written instructions obtained and held on file covering the cutting of coupons?
- Are coupon cards under the control of persons other than those assigned to coupon cutting?
- Are pledged deposit accounts properly coded to negate unauthorized withdrawal of funds?
- Are acknowledgments received for pledged deposits held at other banks?
- Is an officer's approval needed before collateral can be released or substituted?

5. Review processes in the following areas:

- Are acceptance record copies, own acceptances discounted (purchased), and acceptances of other banks purchased safeguarded during banking hours and locked in the vault overnight?
- Are blank (pre-signed) customer drafts properly safeguarded?
- Are any acceptance fee rebates approved by an officer?
- Does the bank have an internal review system that:
  - • Re-examines collateral and supporting documentation held for negotiability and proper assignment?
  - • Test checks values assigned to collateral at frequent intervals?
  - • Determines whether lending officers are periodically advised of maturing bankers' acceptances or acceptance lines?
- Does the bank's acceptance filing system identify each acceptance (e.g., by consecutive numbering and applicable letter of credit) to provide a proper audit trail?

Personnel

Conclusion: Management and personnel (do/do not) display a fundamental understanding of concepts applicable to bankers' acceptances.

Objective: To determine whether management and personnel possess and display acceptable knowledge and technical skills in managing risks inherent in bankers' acceptances, given the size and complexity of the bank.

1. Assess management's skills and knowledge related to bankers' acceptances based on conclusions developed while performing these procedures.

2. Review the bank's training and continuing education program as it relates to the bankers' acceptance department.

Controls

Conclusion: Management (has/has not) established effective control systems for bankers' acceptances.

Objective: To determine whether effective control systems have been established for bankers' acceptances.

1. Assess the effectiveness of the loan review function in identifying risk in bankers' acceptance financing. Consider in the assessment the:

    *   Scope of the review.
    *   Frequency of reviews.
    *   Qualifications of loan review personnel.
    *   Examination findings.

2. Review the most recent loan review report for bankers' acceptances. Determine whether management has appropriately addressed concerns and areas of unwarranted risk.

3. Assess the adequacy of the internal/external audit function with regards to bankers' acceptances. Consider in the assessment the:

- Scope of the audit.
- Frequency of audits.
- Qualifications of audit personnel.

4. Review the most recent audit report for bankers' acceptances. Determine whether management has appropriately addressed noted deficiencies.

5. Determine whether management information systems have the capacity to capture essential information and provide meaningful reports.

Conclusion Procedures

Objective: Prepare written conclusion comments and communicate findings to management. Review findings with EIC before discussion with management.

1. Provide the EIC with brief conclusions regarding:

   - Quantity of risk.
   - Quality of risk management.
   - Any concerns or recommendations.
   - Any classified assets, special mention assets, credit documentation exceptions, or collateral exceptions.

2. For any risk identified while performing the foregoing procedures, determine its impact on aggregate risk and the direction of risk. Examiners should refer to guidance provided under the OCC's risk assessment programs for large banks or community banks.

   - Risk Categories: Strategic, Transaction, Compliance, Credit, Liquidity, Price, Foreign Exchange, Reputation.
   - Risk Conclusions: High, Moderate, or Low.
   - Risk Direction: Increasing, Stable, or Declining.

3. Determine, in consultation with the EIC, whether the risks identified are significant enough to merit bringing them to the board's attention in the report of examination. If so, prepare items for inclusion under the heading "Matters Requiring Board Attention" (MRBA). MRBAs should cover practices that:

   - Deviate from sound fundamental principles and are likely to result in financial deterioration if not addressed.
   - Result in substantive noncompliance with laws.

   MRBAs should discuss:

   - Causes of the problem.
   - Consequences of inaction.
   - Management's commitment to corrective action.

- The time frame for corrective action and persons responsible for such action.

4. Discuss findings with management, including:

   - The quantity of risk assumed by the bank from bankers' acceptances.
   - The quality of the bank's system to manage the risk of bankers' acceptances.
   - The adequacy of written policies and compliance with laws and regulations.
   - Comments for inclusion in the report of examination.
   - The adequacy of information on bankers' acceptances available to management and the board of directors.

5. As appropriate, prepare a brief comment for inclusion in the report of examination.

   - Adequacy of policies, processes, personnel, and control systems.
   - Any deficiencies reviewed with management and any remedial actions recommended.

6. Prepare a memorandum and update work programs with any information that will facilitate future examinations.

7. Update the OCC's electronic information system and any applicable report of examination schedules or tables.

8. Organize and reference working papers in accordance with OCC guidance.

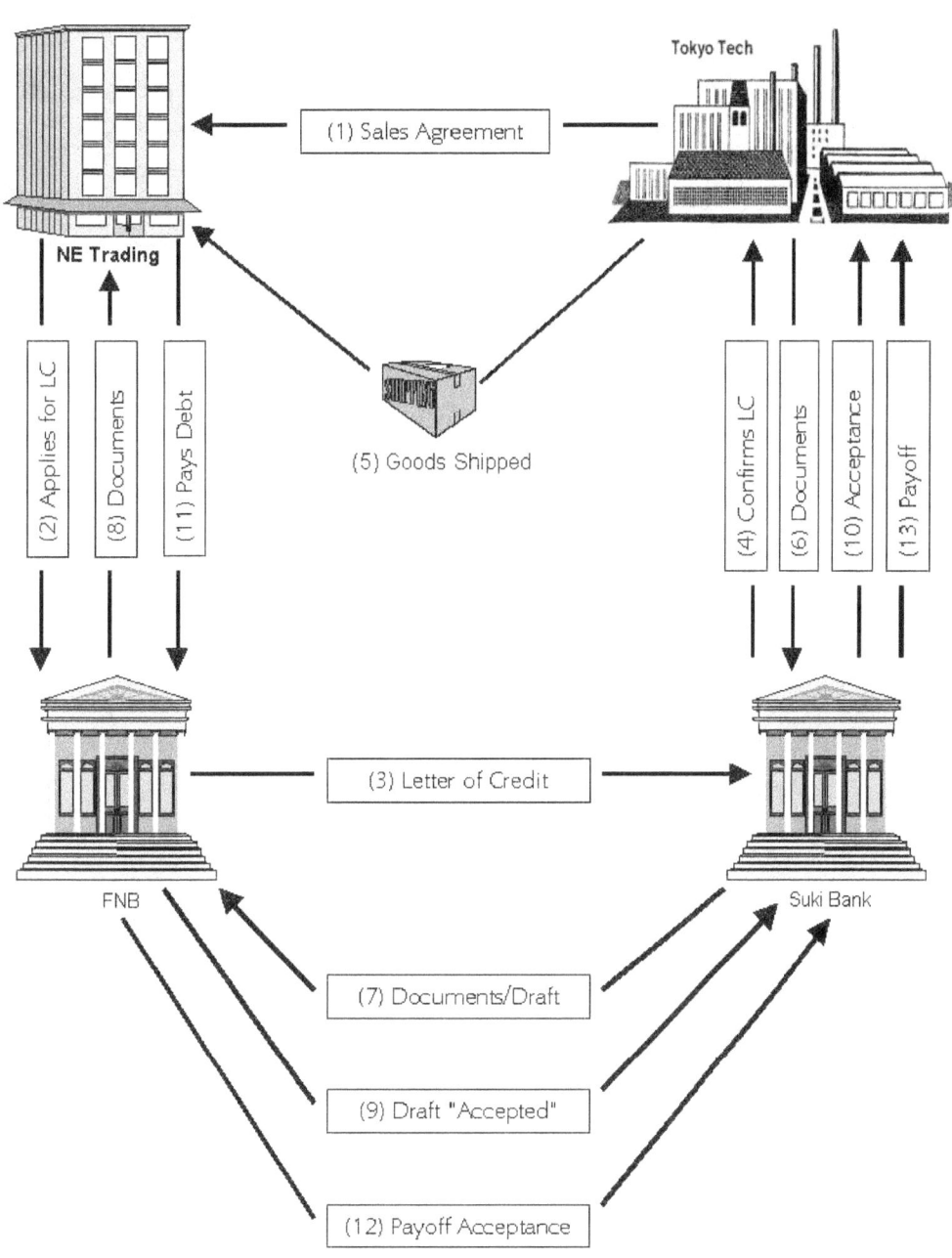

Acceptance of Drafts and Bills of Exchange
Laws   12 USC 372

Acceptance of Drafts for Furnishing Dollar Foreign Exchange
Laws   12 USC 373

Acceptances Used in Financing Credit Transactions
Regulations   12 CFR 7.1007

Bankers' Acceptances: Definition of Participations
Regulations   12 CFR 250.165

Lending Limits • Bankers' Acceptances
Laws   12 USC 84
Regulations   12 CFR 32.3

Transactions with Affiliates • Participations
Laws   12 USC 371c